The Medium Uniform PKW of the German Wehrmacht 1937-1945

A convertible as a commander's car. It is not clear whether the vehicle was built by Gläser of Dresden or Erdmann & Rossi.

Dr. Hans-Georg Mayer-Stein

Schiffer Military/Aviation History
Atglen, PA

Caption will be generated from photocopy.

Bibliography

Bunke, Siegfried, "Die mittleren Einheits-PKWs der ehemaligen deutschen Wehrmacht", in Fahrzeug 2/90, 3/90.

Etzold, Hans-Rüdiger; Rother, Ewald; and Erdmann, Thomas, "Im Zeichen der vier Ringe 1873-1945".

Frank, Reinhard, "Personen-Kraftwagen der Wehrmacht", Friedberg/TS, 1993.

Oswald, Werner, "Kraftfahrzeuge und Panzer der Reichswehr, Wehrmacht und Bundeswehr", Stuttgart, 1973. "Alle Horch-Automobil 1900-1945", Stuttgart, 1979.

Translated from the German by Ed Force

Printed in China.
ISBN: 0-7643-0570-0

This book was originally published under the title,
Waffen Arsenal-Der Mittlere Einheits-PKW der Deutschen Wehrmacht 1937-1945
by Podzun-Pallas Verlag.

We are interested in hearing from authors with book ideas on related topics.

Spielberger, Walter J., "Die Motorisierung der Deutschen Reichswehr 1920-1935", Stuttgart, 1979.

Stühlemmer, Rupert, "The coachwork of Erdmann and Rossi, Berlin", London.

Photo Credits and Information

Automobilmuseum August Horch, Zwickau, Jürgen Pönisch
Auto-Union GmbH, Ingolstadt
Echart Bartels, Ronnenberg bei Hannover
Siegfried Buncke, Duisburg
Carsten Messer, Braunschweig
Podzun-Pallas-Verlag Archives
Author's Archives
Munin-Verlag

Published by Schiffer Publishing Ltd.
4880 Lower Valley Road
Atglen, PA 19310
Phone: (610) 593-1777
FAX: (610) 593-2002
E-mail: Schifferbk@aol.com
Please write for a free catalog.
This book may be purchased from the publisher.
Please include $3.95 postage.
Try your bookstore first.

From the Kübelwagen to the Uniform PKW

In the early twenties, the Reichswehr had to get along with stock passenger cars, for the financial health of both the military budget and the automobile firms was poor, what with the results of the inflation, and this made the development of special off-road vehicles unthinkable.

In procuring the vehicles, the responsible offices of the Reichswehr, for reasons of economy, gave preference to cars of the medium displacement class. To make the cars suitable for military use, certain modifications of the chassis and bodywork were made, such as reducing the gear ratios, strengthening the suspension, installing a locking differential and increasing ground clearance (larger wheels, relocating the exhaust system). Above all, though, open bodies were preferred, with a simple tent roof and rolled-up side curtains.

The designing of such passenger cars modified for military purposes was done by the Reichswehr in cooperation with the German automobile firms. A number of German chassis builders were given the job of building the chassis, with only Auto-Union (Horch and Wanderer) and Mercedes-Benz producing completed "Kübelwagen", as they were called because of the unusual bowl shape of the seats. Horch even rebuilt the noble eight-cylinder Type 853, a top-class car, as a light open Kübelwagen. These vehicles, often disguised as off-road sports cars, were subjected to rigorous testing by the Reichswehr, in order to test their loadability and capability for use; the results were generally satisfactory, even though these open Kübelwagen could not compare with the off-road capability of all-wheel-drive vehicles.

Of course, the great variety of types was a major disadvantage, since the individual commanders usually favored local manufacturers. In addition, cars built for the trade usually undergo frequent model changes, which then affected the corresponding Kübelwagen series as well.

The already long-envisioned goal of a standardized military car had to be taken seriously as of 1933, for Hitler placed the highest value on fast motorized army units in his rebuilding of the military forces. For the designing of off-road-capable vehicles, the Army Weapons Office established guidelines and specifications, including all-wheel drive and steering, locking differentials, low gear ratios for improved climbing and scrambling ability, high ground clearance, protection of sensitive parts, and good fording ability.

The HWA foresaw three "uniform chassis", for a light, medium and heavy passenger vehicle. Through standardization, norming and typification, simplicity of manufacturing and spare-parts procurement were to be achieved. In order to assure the supply of spare parts—in the event of one manufacturing site being destroyed—and to be independent of one manufacturer's special conditions or the possible unexpected difficulties of concentrated production, various firms were given contracts for the uniform chassis. For the production of the light uniform PKW, contracts went to Stoewer (Stettin), BMW (Munich) and Hanomag (Hannover). Responsible for manufacturing the medium E-PKW chassis were Horch (Zwickau), Wanderer (Siegmar/Saxony) and Opel (Rüsselsheim). The heavy off-road E-PKW was built by Horch and Ford.

A division staff on the march with Kfz. 15.

Prerequisites and Development by Horch

The focal point of production, particularly of the medium class, was at Horch. One must, of course, consider their competition with Mercedes-Benz. Klaus Detlof von Oertzen, then the managing director of Auto Union and responsible for its connections with the Nazi Party, recalled: "The firm of Daimler-Benz enjoyed special connections with the German government. They were strengthened even more in that the Mercedes representative Werlin took special care of Party business. He repeatedly made it known to me that the intervention of our Auto-Union cars did not suit him at all, and that Daimler-Benz had a right to receive particularly preferential treatment".

Business with the authorities was slow for Horch and Wanderer, even though it picked up increasingly between 1935 and 1939. Only DKW of the Auto-Union firms was able to profit to a great degree from official business—the small front-drive cars and motorcycles received frequent orders.

Very much greater than the business of Horch and Wanderer with government agencies were their orders from the Army. A comparison of the figures of October 31, 1938 makes this very clear:

Army Contracts (Auto Union)	8435 vehicles
Government contracts	115 vehicles

The Army business was profitable, for the Army Weapons Office was responsible for the costs of designing special military vehicles. Thus there developed an intensive collaboration between the Wehrmacht and Auto Union. The partner of the Horch Works was the Motor Vehicle and Motorization Department of the Official Group for Development and Testing in the Army Weapons Office. The focal points of the developmental work were: all-wheel drive, all-wheel steering, chassis for armored scout cars, off-road-capable medium and heavy personnel cars. Horch was a leader in the designing of these cars.

Until the introduction of the Medium Uniform PKW, the Kübelwagen based on the Horch 830 R was the most suitable medium off-road-capable PKW (Wehrmacht designation Kfz. 15, Telephone and Radio Car); it was a very capable and robust vehicle, though it did lack all-wheel drive for off-road use. The Medium Uniform PKW, built from 1937 on, replaced all the previous Kübelwagen, including the Horch 830 R.

Photographed during a parade in a German city.

Types and Versions

From 1937 on, Horch and Wanderer built chassis for the Medium Uniform PKW. The production designations were Horch 901 and Wanderer 901. The bodies were built by Ambi-Budd (Berlin-Johannisthal) and Gaubschat (Berlin-Neukölln) and then were sent to the chassis builders for final assembly.

As of 1940, Opel was also included in production, since the capacities at Horch and Wanderer were not sufficient. Opel, though, presumably did not build its own chassis (none are listed in the firm's statistics), but had the raw chassis delivered, and only afterward were they designated as Opel chassis. The Uniform PKW was assembled in the Opel factory in Brandenburg, although the cars bore the type label "Adam Opel AG, Rüsselsheim".

Among the troops, the Medium Uniform PKW was almost always referred to simply as "Horch", regardless of where the vehicle had been built.

As to the engines:

The V-8 Horch engine in the Horch and Wanderer 901 was taken from regular production. The Horch Works had expanded their car program downward in 1933 with a "small" Horch as a "thrifty version"; along with the Nobel class with five-liter V-8 engines (100 HP), there now appeared the Horch Type 830 with three- and later 3.5-liter engines (75 HP). After being reworked for specific military purposes, this 80 HP powerplant was used for the Horch-Wanderer 901 Medium Uniform PKW. Since the Horch capacity was too small, Opel not only had to make its production facilities in Brandenburg, where the renowned Blitz was produced, available, but also supply the 3.6-liter engine of the Blitz truck. This six-cylinder, 68 HP engine had proved itself to be very reliable and robust, but fit into the chassis only after large-scale rebuilding.

The gearboxes used by Horch came from the Zahnradfabrik Friedrichshafen (ZF) and from Prometheus (two different versions of each with different ratios); those used in the Opel Type mP I, as the Kfz 15 was officially known, exclusively from ZF. The intermediate gear ratio (road vs. off-road gears) were shifted by a second shift lever. The differentials were also of varying origin (ZF or Rheinmetall),, likewise the steering (ZF or Münz).

The original goals, namely uniformity of components for practicality, cost-cutting, simplification of spare-part supply and easy interchanging of parts, were still far from being attained. With the variety of the most different components, the troops faced the problem of higher repair expenditures. Gearboxes, steering, engines, etc., could either not be exchanged at all or only under difficult, highly complicated conditions. The supplying of spare parts was also made more difficult. Then too, abandoned vehicles could not always be used as sources of parts. For every storekeeper sergeant, this variety caused insoluble problems.

In any case, the Medium Uniform PKW had been built without the problematic all-wheel steering, for unexpected but sensible reasons. In the Light Uniform PKW, it had proved to be very susecptible to damage as well as dangerous to drive with.

The Medium Uniform PKW was made with an open body (Kfz 12 in the first series, Kfz 15 with four or six seats and an equipment box as a telephone and radio vehicle, and Kfz 16 as a range-finding car) and a closed body (radio and telephone car, Kfz 17). Among the troops they were all usually called Kfz 15.

Differing statements of numbers manufactured have surfaced: The Horch factory records show certain differences, since at one time the produced vehicles were counted, while in other [p. 6] statistics the delivered vehicles were noted. The statistics at Wanderer look even worse, because the factory records were taken over by the Dresden State Archives some years ago and are presently unavailable. At Opel there are absolutely no statistics for assembled chassis or engines available. Thus one must rely heavily on estimates, according to which Horch built 13,902, Wanderer 12,298 and Opel several thousand chassis.

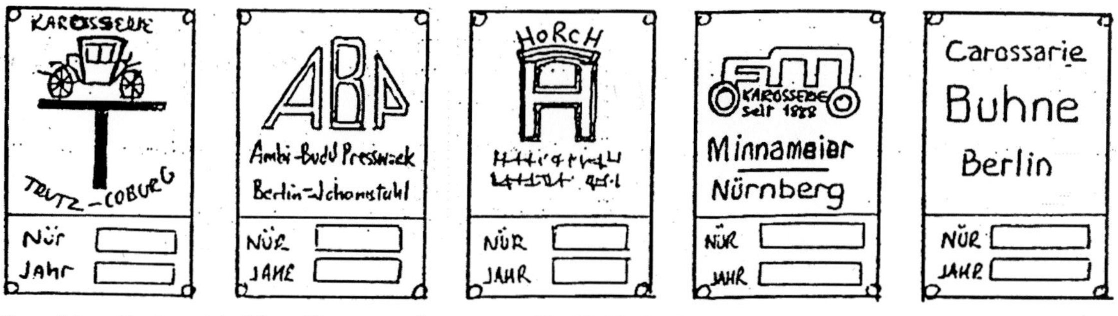

Type plates of bodywork builders. These manufacturers are identifiable through existing vehicles, but there were also Seegers of Leipzig, Linke-Hofmann Werke AG of Breslau, Deisner & Son of Anhalt, and Gläser of Dresden.

Very small numbers (about fifty) of Medium Uniform PKW chassis were also fitted with convertible bodies made by Gläser in Dresden.

In these comfortable cars, the doors were attached to the B-columns and equipped with cranked windows. In addition, they had a complete rear luggage compartment. The convertibles also had a full-width windshield, upholstered seats and a few other refinements. The vehicles by Gläser can be recognized by the chrome strip along the belt line. Since most of these cars were assigned to high officers or commanders, several were also equipped with armor plate.

All these convertibles had a more powerful Horch V-8 engine displacing 3.8 liters and prodicung 90 HP at 3600 rpm. Along with the rarities by Gläser, there were also a few one-off models: a convertible by Erdmann and Rossi with six seats and three side windows, a four-door sedan that was used by the German embassy in Moscow, as well as a few open cars with platforms for filming. The convertibles with spare wheels were also one-offs.

The first versions of 1937 had short front fenders; they also lacked bumpers and boxes for tire chains. These vehicles existed with and without side spare wheels. Very soon all the cars were fitted with front bumpers, and the fenders were extended to them.

Aside from the very few early examples, the differences between an older and a newer version are as follows: The older vehicles can be recognized very easily by the side spare wheels. They had standard hubcaps as well as boxes for tire chains. The engine hoods originally had cooling flaps, and later louvers, on their upper parts, ahead of the windshield.

The striking, turnable support or spare wheels were meant to prevent a car from getting stuck in rough terrain. This design, though, limited the inside space so much that the newer version, the Type 40 built from 1940 on, had only one spare wheel in the interior, behind the driver. Further characteristics of the newer version are central lubrication, a two-piece toolbox cover (previously one-piece), the filler cap for the main fuel tank moved to the outside right, the hubcaps eliminated. As of January 1942 the vehicles were also fitted with off-road axle reinforcements and additional springs.

Here mines are being removed while the rest of the company continues to advance quickly. A Kfz 15 in the French campaign, 1940.

Hard tasks for driver and car in roadless areas in Russia. A Kfz 15 fords a river.

Experience in Action

The Medium Uniform PKW was naturally not free of faults, but it proved itself better than the light and heavy Uniform PKW. Both the Horch and the opel engines were rugged and ran reliably.

Not infrequently, though, there was damage to the wheel suspension, the driveshafts, springs, locking differentials and driveshafts during extreme conditions in Russia. And here a serious weakness of the cars was evident: The spare parts of the various types were either not interchangeable at all or only with great difficulty.

Another serious problem, in fact, was the great amount of servicing. There were 100 (!) lubrication points to be greased. The older cars with support axles were only in part equipped with central lubrication.

A further problem was the high weight: 2.7 tons empty for the Kübelwagen, three tons for the convertible and closed versions with radio equipment. The engine thus had a lot to move, especially in rough country. This also meant high fuel consumption for the cars: 26 liters on the road, 36 off the road. With the Wehrmacht's chronic fuel shortage, this was a big problem.

It was thus only natural that their production was slowed down in 1942 and halted completely in 1943 (the exact date cannot be determined). In addition, the inexpensive, light, simple and yet reliable and off-road-capable VW Kübelwagen had meanwhile reached most troop units in goodly numbers. The Wehrmacht now had a really ideal off-road passenger vehicle that proved itself superbly in all theaters of war.

Picture 35. Chassis with Opel Powerplant

1. Towing hook
2. Exhaust tailpipe
3. Float for fuel gauge
4. Spare fuel tank
5. Fuel filler cap
6. Upper [Lenker]
7. Spring mounts
8. Needle driveshaft
9. Rear axle drive
10. Road wheel
11. Shock absorber
12. Hydraulic brake line
13. Brake cable
14. Main fuel tank
15. Battery
16. Driveshaft (from 2-4WD gearbox to rear axle)
17. Spare wheel mount
18. Spare wheel
19. 2-4WD gearshift
20. Main gearshift
21. Hand brake lever
22. Steering wheel
23. Brake oil duct
24. 2-4WD gearbox cooler
25. 2-4WD gearbox
26. Hand brake cable
27. Driveshaft (from main to 2-4WD gearbox
28. Gearbox shaft
29. Driveshaft (from 2-4WD gearbox to front axle)
30. Air filter
31. Ignition coil
32. Distributor
33. Fuel pump
34. Air intake duct
35. Cooling water duct with thermometer attachment
36. Water hose connector
37. Radiator
38. [Wind wing? not on picture]
39. Tow hook
40. Brake oil line divider

Horch Medium Pkw Type 901.

Convertible with and without spare wheels.

Convertible with spare wheels.

For the pictures on these two pages:
Six-seater convertible on the chassis of the Medium Uniform PKW Horch Type 901. The vehicle was said to have been built for Hitler and thus had a windshield of armored glass. The right front seat can be folded up so that one could stand there during a drive. A special "extra" was a pistol holder with two magazines in the back. The car was painted the usual Wehrmacht gray color but had blue leather upholstery inside.

The pictures on this page show German units that returned to their homeland in the summer of 1940, after the western campaign. The troops are parading with Horch Uniform PKW.
Left: in Krefeld.

In Münster.

In Hamm.

Inspection of a motorized unit at the market place of a small German city shortly before service in the Sudetenland.

A division transferred to East Prussia is greeted enthusiastically by the local population.

In the African campaign, the gray Wehrmacht color proved to be very disadvantageous. Therefore these Uniform PKWs were camouflaged with lime. In some places, tactical markings show through. Besides the swastika flagpole, the vehicle carries a battalion marker and a horseshoe. In addition, washbowls were attached.

A war correspondent takes dramatic pictures of the African campaign. A German vehicle column with Horch Kübelwagen in a cloud of desert dust.

A light division on the march. Between the Schützenpanzerwagen and the motorcycles are several Horch Kübelwagen. Africa, 1941.

Through Romania, Bulgaria and Yugoslavia the Leibstandarte Adolf Hitler SS Division marches into Greece. A Kfz 15 leads motorcycle riflemen on the advance.

A Horch Kübelwagen on the city square in Zamosc.

Many Medium Uniform PKWs)Kfz 15) served as off-road command cars at all levels of command. This is the car of a commanding general (KG)—note the flag on the left front fender.

The British regarded the blowing up of important roads as the only means of stopping the German advance in Greece. This picture shows what a help the side support wheels could be in rough country.

The pictures on this page show scenes from the advance into the Soviet Union in the summer of 1941. Above, a vehicle convoy in the dust, with the renowned "G" of the Guderian Panzer Group on the fender; below, officers with their parked Kfz 15 at the side of the advance route.

The SS "Grossdeutschland" Division with Uniform PKWs, Kübelwagen in front, box (radio) vans in back.

Motorized units of the SS "Das Reich" Division.

A motorcycle rifle battalion uses a railroad line as an advance route in the direction of the important city of Kiev. A Kfz 15 leads the way.

Wheeled and tracked vehicles on the advance route during a jam before a bridge.

On the 28th of [month omitted], Reval fell into German hands. The Horch Kübelwagen of an infantry regiment drives through the just-captured city.

A Medium Uniform PKW drives through an archway, probably the gate of a rich landowner's estate. The small guardhouse indicates that the staff of a German division is based here.

Two Uniform PKWs under a thick cloud of dust in the Rava-Ruska area.

Orders at the roadside. Oberstleutnant Ritter von Hauenschild with officers and NCOs.

Above and below: The Commander of the 4th Panzer Army, Generaloberst Hoth, at the command post in Kasanka in June 1942. The pictures show the commander's car, a Horch convertible.

The convertible of Generalmajor Schelle (Commander of the 9th Panzer Division) at their Schidra post in August 1942.

A pause in a march is used for taking photographs.

A German unit has stopped at a crossroads. An interesting variety of vehicles, including the Uniform PKW.

Three soldiers pose for a photo next to their Horch Kübelwagen.

Left: A convertible with a support wheel, Kfz 21.

Right: Generaloberst Hoth, Commander of Panzer Group 3, stands in his Horch Uniform PKW during the combat around Moscow in the winter of 1941.

Left: A Medium Uniform PKW crossing the Düna in the summer of 1941.

Right: Summer 1941: the Uniform PKW of a division staff.

Left: The autumn mud season begins!

Above: Two Uniform PKWs at the Ostrov depot, summer 1941.

Right: A scrapped Medium Uniform PKW and a Russian KW 1 tank, whose armor withstood everything but the 88 mm Flak shells.

Above: Slow going over a corduroy road.

Left: A commander's car has broken through the logs.

Pictures taken near Linez during the mud season, October 1941. A rough road for men and machines.

Repairing the commander's car.

Below: A downright artistic "pit" for servicing.

Winter camouflage often had to be put on in a hurry. The vehicles were hastily covered in chalk white with brushes, brooms, scrubbers, rags, sponges or even bare hands.

These two Uniform PKWs have already received their "winter coat"; the VW Kübelwagen between them has not.

Generaloberst Model gives commands for the action of his units, here the Kdr. Panzer Unit, from a Horch convertible.

Feldmarschall Schörner visits the command post of a division in his Horch Kübelwagen, May 1944.

Right: The Commanding General of the Waffen-SS, General Hausser, visits the "Das Reich" Division in his Horch.

Left: A commander in his Uniform PKW.

Right: A commander's convertible at the Schidra position near Schilkovo, the scene of hard fighting in August 1942.

A Medium Uniform PKW of the Luftwaffe, with a Hanomag behind it.

The "Citadel" attack has begun. A heavy grenade-launcher battalion is seen on the advance route in July 1943.

After scouring the village, the men gather again at their vehicles. Here are two Medium Uniform PKWs, with a "Russian Ford" behind them.

The enemy tries to dismount and is pursued by PKWs and tanks.

An Army Uniform Kübelwagen stuck in Russian mud; note the civilian Berlin license plate.

The Army withdraws in the spring of 1944, fighting not only against the enemies that pursue them closely and attack their flanks, but also against mud and rain. Officers and men of a Luftwaffe unit push a commander's car through the mud.

Schützenpanzerwagen and Horch-Kübel of a Waffen-SS unit stuck in the mud.

An Assault Gun III, Type F, and a Horch Kübelwagen leave deep ruts in the mud. The gray paint of the Horch with Luftwaffe plates is smeared with mud. The Stu. G. III is using eastern tracks, and carries spare links on the rear. Spring 1943.

Technical Data

Chassis:

Length	mm	4695
Width	mm	1840
Wheelbase	mm	3100
Front track	mm	1532
Rear track	mm	1532
Clearance under front axle	mm	250
Clearance under rear axle	mm	160
Clearance fully loaded	mm	160
Front overhang angle ca.	degr	57
Rear overhang angle ca.	degr	40
Ready-to-run chassis weight with two-wheel steering	kg	2000

Performance of Loaded Vehicle

Top speed	ca. kph	96
Minimum speed in first gear	kph	4
Climbing ability fully loaded	ca,	63% (3300 kg)
Fording ability	mm	550
Turning circle, 2-wheel steering	m	14.0
Range on road	ca.	km 400
Oil consumption per 100 km	ca. ltr	0.2
Fuel consumption per 100 km	ca. ltr	24.5

Engine Data: Performance Figures

Number of cylinders		8
Engine position		front
Displacement	cc	3547
Bore	mm	78
Stroke	mm	92
Top allowable engine speed	rpm	3600
Normal HP at rpm		30/3600
Compression ratio		6.3

Engine Data:	Design
Functioning	4-stroke
Material of crankcase	special cast iron
Material of crankshaft	BSF.Duro
Material of cyl. head	special cast iron
Engine mounting	3-point swinging
Cylinder arrangement	66-degree V-8
Number of cylinder heads	2
Number of crankshaft bearings	3
Number of camshafts	1
Camshaft drive	triple chain with tension & adjustment
Number of intake valves per cylinder	1
Number of exhaust valves per cylinder	1
Valve arrangement	lying
Valve activation	rocker arms & rollers
Pistons by	Melson-Breitplatten or Nüral

Piston play	mm	0.94
Number of piston rings		2
Number of oil rings		1
Oil cleaning		Mahle-Nebenstrom U/H 1 filter
Oil cooler		none
Compression space in cylinder head		cc 80

Clutch

Clutch type	Single-plate dry
Clutch play on foot pedal	25-30
Number of clutch springs	9

Cooling

Type	Pump circulation
Type of pump	Laminated flat
Driven by	Camshaft
Valve driven by	Belt
Temperature indication	By hand through flap

Fuel System:

Fuel tank location	Center of car, in frame
Reserve tank location	Rear of car, in frame
Fuel pump	Solex membrane
Fuel filter	Plate filter
Pump drive	Rod from camshaft

Carburetor:

Number of carburetors		2
Type of carburetors	Solex flat 30 BFM	
Air filter diameter	mm	27
Main duct		130 x 51
Idle duct		0.45
Starting mechanism	Built-in starter	
Activation	Cable	
Air filter type	Mahle centrifugal	

Capacities:

Fuel: main tank	ltr	70
reserve tank	ltr	40

Oil:

Motor oil in crankcase	ltr	6.5
in central lubricating housing	ltr	0.75
Oil in main gearbox	ltr	2.0
Oil in 2-4WD gearbox	ltr	2.0
Oil in front axle drive	ltr	1.25
Oil in rear axle drive	ltr	1.25
Oil in steering gear	ltr	0.78
Brake fluid in reservoir	ltr	0.75

Water:

Radiator & motor contents	ltr	20.5

Air:	atm	2.75

Main Gearbox:

	KB 30 D	Promth.
Type		AGN 18
Ratios: reverse	6.75	5.1
first gear	5.48	5.47
second gear	3.11	2.81
third gear	1.3	1.56
fourth gear	1.0	1.0
off-road gear		- -
2-4WD box: on-road		1.097
off-road		1.69
Lubrication		sprayed oil

Front Axle:

Front axle drive	cone wheel plate wheel
Gleason gearing	5.375
Klingenberg gearing	5.285
Type of equalizer	cone wheel

Front Half-shafts:

Manufacturer	Horch
Inner bearings	Needle
Outer bearings	Double joint
Length equalizers	Wedge-shaped
Inner lubrication	By hand
Outer lubrication	Oil bath

Front Wheels:

Wheel size	flat	6"-18
Tire size		190 x 18
Tire pressure	atm	2.75
Front spring type	coil	
number		4
Front shock absorbers	Boge & F&S	
Number per wheel		2

Rear Axle:

Rear drive type	conical plate
Gleason gear ratio	5.375
Klingenberg gear ratio	5.285
Equalizer type	Rheinmetall self-locking

Rear half-shafts:

Manufacturer	Horch
Inner bearings	Needle
Outer bearings	Needle
Length equalizer	Wedge-shaped
Inner lubrication	Oiling by hand
Outer lubrication	Oiling by hand

Rear wheels:

Wheel size	Flat	6"-18
Tire size Off-road		190-18
Tire pressure	atm	2.75
Rear spring type	Coil	
Number		4

Here it was only a rainstorm from which the two soldiers sought shelter under the Horch.

Rear shock absorbers	Boge & F&S	
Number per wheel		2

Brakes:

Foot brake type	Hydraulic drum	
Braked wheels		4
Brake fluid reservoir	On firewall	
Brake drum diameter		350 mm
Brake width		50 mm
Hand brake type	Mechanical cable	
Braked wheels		2 rear

Steering:

Manufacturer	ZF license Ross or Fulmina Münz	
Type	Worm gear or spindle	
Steering wheel full turns		3.75-4
Greatest extent of lever		76
Wheel diameter	mm	450

Frame:

Frame type	Welded box	
Number of front tow hooks		2
Number of rear tow hooks		2
Couplings		1
Coupling height above ground	mm	600

Lubrication:

Central lubrication made by	Vogel	
Filler locations	Under engine hood	
Number of lubricating points		25

Spare Wheel:

Location	in body

Maximum allowable chassis + body weight:

With normal springs	kg	3300
With reinforced springs	kg	3750
Maximum front axle pressure		
With normal springs	kg	1400
With reinforced springs	kg	1650
Maximum rear axle pressure		
With normal springs	kg	1900
With reinforced springs	kg	2100

Electrical System:

Ignition type	Battery
Number of coils	2
Type	Bosch TK 12/1
Distributor	made by Bosch
Type	VGH 8, ARS 124
Ignition type	Vertical wave
Ignition setting	Automatic
Spark plug type	Bosch W 145 T 22

Generator:

Manufacturer	Bosch
Type	RKCK 130/12, 825 R 1
Drive	Belt from crankshaft

Starter:

Manufacturer	Bosch
Type	EJD 1.8/12R4

Power Transmission of the Medium PKW (Type 901):

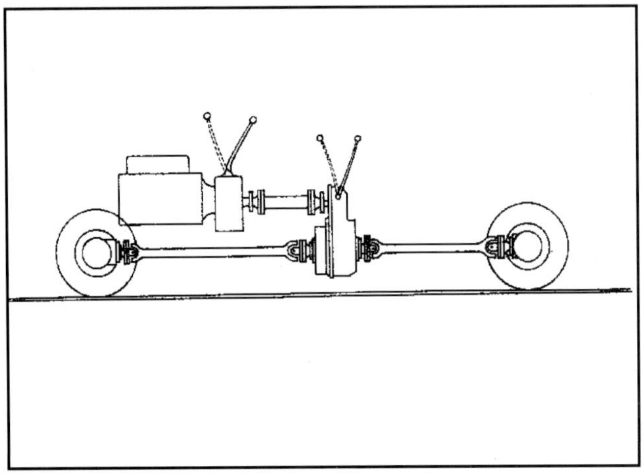

1. Between main and 2-4WD gearboxes: Driveshaft witrh one forward and one rear joint.
2. Between 2-4WD gearbox and rear axle drive: Driveshaft with one forward and one rear joint.

[page 45]

3. Between 2-4WD gearbox and front axle drive: Driveshaft with one forward and one rear joint.
4. Between front axle drive and left/right wheel hubs: Half-shafts with joint on axle, double joint in housing.
5. Between rear axle drive and left/right wheel hubs: Half-shafts with two joints.

Chassis and Engine Serial Numbers

Type 901, 3.5 liter, 80 HP (8-cylinder), with support axle, 1937-1940

Chassis # 10,001-14,162 Engine # 910,001-919,999
Wanderer, Siegmar: 4162 units
Chassis # 20,001-27,869 Engine # 919,100-919,2389
Horch, Zwickau: 7869 units

Type 40, 3.5 liter, 80 HP (8-cylinder), without support axle

Chassis # 40,001-48,136 Engine # 919,2374-919,9999
Engine # 901,0001-901,9999
Wanderer, Siegmar, 8136 units (1940-42)

Chassis # 50,001-57,033 Engine # 902,0000-902,9999
Horch, Zwickau: 7033 units (1940-43)

Type 40, 3.8 liter, 90 HP (8 cylinder), Komm convertible, 1940-42

Chassis # 51,375-56,108 Engine # 381,0001... ca. 55 units

Type mP I 3.6 liter, 68 HP (6 cylinder, 1940-42 or 43)

Chassis # 30,001... (no statistics), Opel/Brandenburg
Several thousand units

Instrument panel of a command car, vehicle shown on page 1.

Rear view of a Medium Uniform PKW; note the covers of the side support wheels.

The restored Kfz 15 of a Norse collector; see also front cover.

Interior views of a restored radio car.

GERMAN TRUCKS & CARS IN WWII VOL.VIII FORD AT WAR Horst Scheibert.

Size: 8 1/4" x 11 3/4"
48 pages
soft cover
b/w photographs, line drawings
ISBN: 0-88740-480-4

$9.95